The
in the Forest

CW01582373

PHASE 3 AND 4

4b

Level 4 – Blue

BookLife Readers

Helpful Hints for Reading at Home

The graphemes (written letters) and phonemes (units of sound) used throughout this series are aligned with Letters and Sounds. This offers a consistent approach to learning whether reading at home or in the classroom. Books levelled as 'a' are an introduction to this band. Readers can advance to 'b' where graphemes are consolidated and further graphemes are introduced.

HERE IS A LIST OF NEW GRAPHEMES FOR THIS PHASE OF LEARNING. AN EXAMPLE OF THE PRONUNCIATION CAN BE FOUND IN BRACKETS.

Phase 3			
j (jug)	v (van)	w (wet)	x (fox)
y (yellow)	z (zoo)	zz (buzz)	qu (quick)
ch (chip)	sh (shop)	th (thin/then)	ng (ring)
ai (rain)	ee (feet)	igh (night)	oa (boat)
oo (boot/look)	ar (farm)	or (for)	ur (hurt)
ow (cow)	oi (coin)	ear (dear)	air (fair)
ure (sure)	er (corner)		

HERE ARE SOME WORDS WHICH YOUR CHILD MAY FIND TRICKY.

Phase 3 Tricky Words			
he	you	she	they
we	all	me	are
be	my	was	her

Phase 4 Tricky Words			
said	were	have	there
like	little	so	one
do	when	some	out
come	what		

HERE ARE SOME WORDS THAT MIGHT NOT YET BE FULLY DECODABLE.

Challenge Words			
whispers	come		

TOP TIPS FOR HELPING YOUR CHILD TO READ:

- Allow children time to break down unfamiliar words into units of sound and then encourage children to string these sounds together to create the word.
- Encourage your child to point out any focus phonics when they are used.
- Read through the book more than once to grow confidence.
- Ask simple questions about the text to assess understanding.
- Encourage children to use illustrations as prompts.

PHASE 3 AND 4

4b

This book is a 'b' level and is a blue level 4 book band.

The Trolls in the Forest

Written by
Emilie Dufresne

Illustrated by
Cassie Gregory

“Ren, do you wish to join me and go down to the forest?” asks Mai.

"I cannot go too far from town. I cannot join you," said Ren.

Mai looks in her pocket. "We will flip this coin. If it is tails, then you join me."

As Mai flips the coin, an owl swoops down and grabs it.

"My coin!" said Mai. "We need to keep that owl in sight!"

Mai and Ren run along the trail down to the forest. The owl waits for them.

The owl looks at them and then floats off with the coin in its foot.

"What shall we do?" asks Mai as the owl swoops into the wood.

It is dark in the wood. It smells of soil and a brook runs between the bamboo.

"Owl, can I have my coin back?" asks Mai.
But the owl points its wing to the left...

"Are they... Trolls? How did they get into this wood?" asks Ren.
"Shall we ask them?" said Mai.

The owl sits on a branch looking down at them. "Trolls, how did you get into this wood?" asks Ren.

"We need to go right at the bamboo tree!" said the brown troll, not seeing Mai and Ren.

"No! That is not right, this is," said the red troll. "What is that down there?"

"They can fit in my pocket!" said the brown troll.

The brown troll picks Mai up.
"Do not put her in a pocket!" said Ren.

"Can we keep them as pets?" said the brown troll.
"But the cow is going to be a pet for us," said the red troll.

"Well they can help boil the spuds," said the brown troll.
"Put me down!" said Mai.

"Is it doing a speech?" said the red troll.
"Now, I do not wish to spoil this chat, trolls," said Mai.

"But I need my coin back from that owl. So put me down, right now!" she said, pointing.

The brown troll puts Mai down on the damp soil.

"What will you get us if we let you go?" asks the brown troll.

At that, the owl swoops down and drops the coin into Ren's hand.

"This coin is for you," said Yuki. "It will bring you luck."

"Now go, and do not come back," said Mai. "The trolls are not bright. It is just a coin!" she whispers to Ren.

"Owl, can you bring us back to town?" said Ren.
"What fun we had!" said Mai.

The Trolls in the Forest

1. Why did Ren say he couldn't go with Mai to the forest?

2. What animal did the red troll want to keep as a pet?

   (a) A cow

   (b) A dog

   (c) A snake

3. How do you think Mai felt when the troll picked her up?

4. How did Mai and Ren get back to town?

5. Do you think Mai and Ren tricked the trolls with the coin?

   Can you explain your answer?

©2020 **BookLife Publishing Ltd.**
King's Lynn, Norfolk PE30 4LS

ISBN 978-1-83927-289-9

All rights reserved. Printed in Malaysia.
A catalogue record for this book is available from the British Library.

The Trolls in the Forest
Written by Emilie Dufresne
Illustrated by Cassie Gregory

An Introduction to BookLife Readers...

Our Readers have been specifically created in line with the London Institute of Education's approach to book banding and are phonetically decodable and ordered to support each phase of the Letters and Sounds document.

Each book has been created to provide the best possible reading and learning experience. Our aim is to share our love of books with children, providing both emerging readers and prolific page-turners with beautiful books that are guaranteed to provoke interest and learning, regardless of ability.

BOOK BAND GRADED using the Institute of Education's approach to levelling.

PHONETICALLY DECODABLE supporting each phase of Letters and Sounds.

EXERCISES AND QUESTIONS to offer reinforcement and to ascertain comprehension.

BEAUTIFULLY ILLUSTRATED to inspire and provoke engagement, providing a variety of styles for the reader to enjoy whilst reading through the series.

AUTHOR INSIGHT:
EMILIE DUFRESNE

Born in Québec, Canada, Emilie Dufresne's academic achievements explain the knowledge and creativity that can be found in her books. At a young age, she received the award of Norfolk County Scholar, recognising her top grades in school. At the University of Kent, Emilie obtained a First Class Honours degree in English and American Literature, and was awarded a Masters in The Contemporary with Distinction. She has published over 60 books with BookLife Publishing, in subjects ranging from science to geography, art and sports, and even animals as superheroes! Children enjoy Emilie's books because of the detailed narrative and the engaging way she writes, which always entices children to want to learn more.

PHASE 3 AND 4

4b

This book is a 'b' level and is a blue level 4 book band.